S0-CTT-546

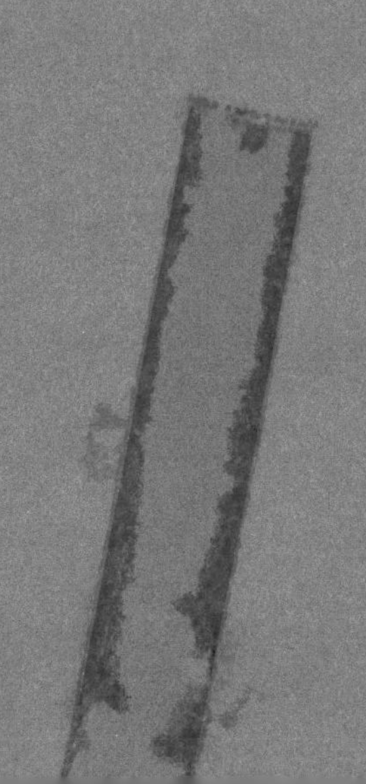

pieces for the old earth man

SEÁN VIRGO | PIECES

for the old earth man

The Sono Nis Press | 1973

Pieces for the Old Earth Man has been published
with the assistance of the Canada Council

Published by
THE SONO NIS PRESS
Delta, British Columbia

Designed and printed in Canada by
MORRISS PRINTING COMPANY LTD.
Victoria, British Columbia

acknowledgements

SOME OF THE POEMS in this book have previously appeared in the following magazines and anthologies:

The Antigonish Review, *The Canadian Forum*, *Cloud Nine: Vancouver Island Poems* (Soft Press), *Contemporary Poetry of B.C. Vol. 1* (Sono Nis), *The Far Point*, *Fiddlehead*, *Poetry Review* and *Wascana Review*.

"Sea Change" was published as a broadsheet by the Sceptre Press, England, in 1971.

Many of these poems have been broadcast on the *Anthology* series of the C.B.C.

contents

one: afagddu

two: yesterday

three: equinox

afagddu

AFAGDDU

They set me to work in the meadow
Diawl it was hot
In the house they chinked glasses

I cut a long swathe down the hedgerow
Prickling with sweat
Hayseeds all over

Even the crickets were sleeping
The earth was loose dust
Pinned down by the stubble

I was weary and far from the evening
Slyly crouched down
Out of sight in the grasses

There on the blade of their sickle
With blood from my thumb
I worked their destruction

SON OF THE MORNING

Lucifer panned for gold all on
The winterbeach, though Mowgli hair
And mean little breasts concealed him.
To the winter colony she was Lucy
From the black hills, poor and dumb
As dirt. She passed among them
Bed to bed and sometimes no cabin
At all. Streaky urchin face
Said nothing to lover or loser. Days
In the pacific drizzle she squatted
Panning out shell from sand, her secret
From the last black grains at the waves'
Edge. And *'ma gold'* was Lucy's
Funny core.

> On Devil's Tower
> they say Old Scratch
> has a smithy waiting
> for firing,
> has a mould waiting
> for a sword of fire.

In the spring time
Three wristwatch hippies raped her down
The end of the beach. She couldn't tower
And split their grovelling backs out of
A thunderclap. It was her purpose,
Though her skinny snatch wrenched
Like a thumbscrew at them. Then
They danced round her, scattered
The dirt from her little leather pouch
All over her, kicked the beach
In her face. Took off. It was
Her purpose. Left her all evening
Into the half-moon, picking gold dust

From her bush.   Sifting the sands
Through her dumb tearstreaks.   *'Ma gold'* . . .

When Lucy's through, in Fall or through
Another winter, that leather bag will lie
On her: a third, fuller breast.   God knows
What they may do to her, trudging back,
Thumbing out to the black hills.   It's her
Purpose.   Lucifer working in his way.

THE HERMIT

I

The air is sweet as
Silver-drip in here.
I've run my mile.
At such times Time
Is not an enemy but
An interval. Confound
The mirror last week
With my dead face
Speaking the calm lie
Into the appalling
White face of prayer.

II

My hunters would starve
In these woods
Who grow clam-fat
On the tide line.
Mobbed by wasps on
This mountain
My hands stank of rabbits' guts.
I hug my bowels tight
Against the rock face
While the mountain tips.
Hurry Time.

III

The tiny balance
Between earth and sky
Laid down in the dewponds.
I am lying: in wait
For a crack in the silver pool
To sneak Time through.
As I am lying

I wonder to the curious
Ears of moss   Am I
Sinking into death
Or into exile?

WHEN MERLIN DIES

Falling back in this room.

Something is happening — but I
Have lost sight of my body:
The cold hulk, the locked ribs.
A mirror clouds through my last
Breath. Something has happened
But I guess crazily and labour
In darkness.
A birth?
Am I
thorn, sprung
From a giant's grave?
Am I
wave, moon-gaffed
Through the straits?
Am I
boulder, lodged by
The ruined hillside?
Am I
mist?
Here
is a clearing.

How long
I am at last
How long
I have become

The chalk down clusters
Round my navel, and white
Like a tiny snake, down there,
That line on the blue turf.

Suppose it is the trail of girls
Colt free and floating green off good hills
To stitch in the wind's web harmony

Of their first dance. Gold silk measures of
Their first dance on the emerald downs.

But the weft tears free from the old wives'
Fingers and mocks the skinny grabbing
Of their arms. It tatters and flaps trails
Of broken girls, laughing in the next
Valley, and whimpers away in the grim
Sockets of the sea cliffs, to no tune.

The gullies crawl all morning
With a boy swarm. They chatter
After jackdaw eggs in the rocks
Of Cat's Castle, until they fall
At noon, borne feather-light and
Hushed towards the waves.

No more
Happy brawls and treasure hunts
And ducking under the blue-eyed
Birds' grey gab. No more chucking
Of stones in the wind's face.

Only,
Caught at wave top, they return
As mariners, sailwrights who
Stitch to the wind's dictation
And so come on. The crow's nest
Sights cliffs at last and out of
One afternoon come strangers
Scaling the downs.

So stiff
In this untuned strength, they clutch
At the echoes of an old dance
And lunge to stop those rents
In the cold wind's fabric.

All in good time.

HAGGARD

He was poised on a high dead branch
And my wings stammered;
I faltered before his lonely strength.

He was aware of me surely
But flickered late for his vantage
And chased me under the red cliff
And matched my weavings along the rocks,
On the doves' path.
The hectic within me of the hunted,
I soared from myself in him
And on the green cliff edge
Assented.

He stooped a yard from me
Above the cliff,
And hopped to me on fisted talons
To cover me with the dark sweep
Of the raptor's wings.
In that shadow of death
I stifled as his softness mated mine
And again.

He whistled to the air and lifted sheer
From my crouched, crushed self,
And slipped down dropping,
And under the cliff swept out again
On the dark wing sweep:
Whistling over the cold fields
Strong and lonely.

While I above, gripping the turf,
Shuddered my feathers smooth
Over the mate-mark
And the indifferent seed.

THE CATCH

Hooked to the wind
And torn down the scream
Of ages —
Disclaim wonder.
No shock — from the random
Of our elements
We rise finally by the rock
Of irony, sole constant.

Yes, for every fish
The lure is stored, until
The plumes' trim, and chance
Of cast and current
At the given place, cement.

In knowledge then
— For those spared
Other ends — the strike is made:
The fish, his own ironist,
Rising to snap at recognition
And hold fast.

It is surrender though
That the live love unchange:
The deep waiting
Wills away will.

Somewhere for you
There waits the charm
That ties up all. You know
If you shun searching
How through its hiding
It will work to you.

At last take fiercely
For you are giving all. Seizing
That perfect thing

You break the surface;
The line screams; you are
Plucked down the furrowed speedway —
A tiny catch, flashing
And flying
Past unlettered rocks.

NET HAGS

With claw fingers combing out
Dark lanks of water weed
From the morning nets, they remember
The walk one night Black Donal took
Dead moons ago, stepping out
On the silver track to the islands.

SEA CHANGE

Below the gunwale crouched
A little red man, leapt up
Staring when Donal came down
On watch. Stern lantern
Dipping over great shadows
Of iron-hand grapplers. Shook
And pressed the lean body
Against him, fingered
The dark throat. Arched back
On the rail, the wild face
Breathed on Donal's, as through
Its blankness
Death tightened a finger knot.
Two faces at last
Sharing breath, and, recalled
For ever, the flex of eyes
Expiring.
                    Home for winter
Donal put out the lamp
By their bed, knowing his wife.
Always her arched back
Coming against him, the breath
Not his along his face,
Carried him off. The eyes
He knew
Would blast his manhood.

TIME OUT

Down the sands Donal went
In passion, for ghosts bayed
Behind him. Pent hunters they
Hurtled from caves in the years'
Mountain, and mobbed down
His valley, squatting and shifting
At the trees' edge. Donal
Held rage a quiver on the shingle
But the waves marked none
Of that, morgue-still was the air.

Slaps of planking sea by Donal's
Burning feet and the seventh wave
Sluiced out all passion: — Donal
Stood a boneman in the moon-
Picked stones. The beach a frozen
Marathon stretched and the bled
Man slipped off his skin
To dump it over a rock: —
Limp, patch-haired and left
Moon-white.

He joined the cold
Beach company. Sea sound
Lost focus, left only — stepping
Among the stones and skins —
Shy feet of other wraiths
In the hunt's moontime. There
A fox slack and wind-stroked
Lain straight. Donal touched
And tried, fearing a beating
From his grandad's god:

but this
Was beyond that — the fox no murder
From his traps. A sealskin

Snored stiff at the moon and folded
Round him with liver-spots,
A deep tempter. On was a stag
Rock snagged on its velvets; a ripped
Eider and flat dogfish. Night
Lay as long as the new beach
For Donal's part to take
A hundred rank smothers
And freedoms, dipping, or to soar.

All round were his peers, heard
Less than surf and lastly,
An end though no end to sight,
Another nude skin ungainly and white
A girl. Nothing would do.
Turned jealous for his pelt, Donal,
Dashing and jostling through
The changes, heard the beach ground up
And wind bring back the sea loss.

So back, in his chilled skin,
Yet grown hot again, Donal headed
To the tree line. There drove the lame
Pack back 'til the mountain
Should make steeper pitch, and burst
To his wife's bed.

She railed
In cold fear at this drunk, and he
Soothed her, held shoulders though
He shook;
Entering her and thrusting down,
Down into the drumming, dark
Thicket ahead. No end yet or
Alternative, now knowing his skin
Would never fit him well.

SURVEYOR

Stooped in the drizzle
Like an early photographer:
Two legs and three legs
Spying the land's lie.

The rain is beading
On his metal eyepiece;
He turns up his collar
With one hand. He is

The butler at the future's
Keyhole, the Punch and Judy
Man ducked into trouble.
He turns the cold milled screw.

And a rag-Tom like me,
Rain-slinking at the field's
Edge, thinks to slip by.
No chance — he looks up,

Calling out, man to man.
Should have kept moving;
Slouch through October
Thistles, trapped now.

Rain is hair salt
On the lips. "Come on in,"
He grins like a dentist,
"See how she looks."

You guess the tube
Will show you stars
And microbes. Instead
It's hairlines, scales

And the old rain haze
Outside. There's nothing.

"Like this," he moulds you,
Showing you how to see.

At his hand's edge,
Through the slash and brush,
The tumble stack
Of the beechwoods.

"Say when" he says
And the focus storms
At your drinking eye.
There is no *when* anymore.

White wood
Above the stumps
Still rooted and
White cores

Of the slim grey elbows
White tipped
On the snake roots
White wood

And the rain stain
Ochre
The trunks bleeding
Towards you bleeding

The acrid drum
Of the bloodwave coming
Cocking and snatch
In your metalled eye

And "No" you screech,
You hedgerow Jack,
And flap like an old crow
From iron, glass and man.

Under the leaves
You remember what frost

Will be like; you want there
To be smoke when you breathe,

But the rain isn't cold.
"Steady," pleads your January
Skull, "Blood is
Simply a dimension."

But in the rank hand's
Grip you swore
That trees do bleed
That blood is us.

STONEFALL CEMETERY

Walter calls time by the sun,
Never mistaken, tea-break
To knocking-off. The dead
Don't die much in summer
Though the digging is easy,
So I help the old timer.

We plant thrift.
He says, 'A weed is only
A flower you don't want',
Shaking off the dusty,
Pricky forget-me-nots.
And 'One year's weed
Is seven years' seed,'
He says
'You have to tend your choice.'

We lay the forget-me-nots out
Row upon row in the back field
Behind the war graves.
It doesn't take long. In days
We'll prick out seedlings.
There's changes coming.

For their different dead
Last April the synagogue
Bought the back field.
The bulldozers will be trucked in
Soon — next week, Walter says —
To level our tips.
Grass and earth
And rubbish smoothed out:
We'll have to nurse
And dispose somewhere else
After that.
                    Meanwhile we fetch

Musty chrysanths and irises
From the crematorium. Rain-faded
Messages from the living
And the rusty wreath-bones
Go with them. They can rot
There til the lease expires.

On the refuse dump
Against the back wall
The weeds are in lovely riot.

AS THINGS WILL

Here is a dry man in Waterslade,
Turning a corner. Who would guess
Of his staunch back in the high street,
This man is troubled nightly
With hot dreams, this man
Finds daily he must wrestle
With ice in his inkwells?

The cobbles turn his dry steps
Awry, and shuffle beneath bare soles
In his moonlight dreams. They know,
But guard his secrets as things will.

Who knows that his pillow shells out
Whispers of infernal tides
Whirling in his room? Who would believe
That leather office chair
Is a cold-current crow's nest?

Oh the wicked vertiginous
Office clock might tell,
Or the cheap alarm, biding out daylight
To toll his dreams.

But things, unasked, will sham
Senselessness forever.

Yet here is a wet man in Woodhouse
County Asylum, crouched
In a white-wall corner, remote
As a stone from his watchers. Senseless.

They cannot contain him, though:

He is flowing out under the doors,
Filling the halls and running
Cobble-deep down the streets
Of Stonehaven.

I think we should
Tread softly in the gutters if we must
Go up that way. God guards
This tiny flood, soon to run dark
And swift by the town hall windows
Where the dry burghers
Recapitulate.

RUNES FOR ROBIN

Scratch the merryman of mark
Twice he will reel on goat's feet
Stand browsing off willow peel
Green wand all through.

So with his lady marrying
Maid of green to green 'til autumn
Drifts the tides   turned young
She is fay foundering nightmare.

Then the king taller his lieutenant
Long wrestler watched through bars
Songsought found yet faithful
Poison curses the green core.

UNDER THE BOUGH

I

'What have I got in my hand?'
Said the hanging man.
'Nothing that you can show.'
Said the old crow.

'When did they go away?'
'At the break of day.'

'How long will they leave me here?'
'Til the new year.'

'What shall I tell them then?'
' "Return again." '

'Will there be any more?'
'Caw. Caw.'

II

While cuckoo swooped
Over pipit's secret,
Her forger was daubing
The white shell, dreaming
Idly of Cythera.

III

God's eye
Is a cross
Of hand-snapped
Apple twigs,
        Bound round
        And round
        With a web
        Of wool-scraps;
And the temper
Of God's eye

Is meek to the weave
Of our hands.

IV

You, by disdain, gain grace
Of the angel flock dipping
In favour, fickle as amnesty.

You, tracing the leaf-chased
Gunlock, while the doves wheel in
Unwary over the harvest;

You, pursuing your placid
Lifeline, while the maple keys
Spin legions through the sunshafts
Around your downturned
Autumn-haloed head.

V

What thawed my winter dream
In the morning? (Dreams and years
From my store scarcely dwindled,
And my snout in my belly fur.)

The shoots are tight at noon
And the roots malign. I blink out
With my chin on the ditch's lip.

PIECES FOR THE OLD EARTH-MAN . . .

I have inherited
I have inherited
My old lord is dead in exile.
Silly prince, clumsy magician. . . .

. . . .

They say he was let down
Without a pose or bardic
Gesture — only his fallen belly
Stopped digesting. . . .

. . . .

The first time by the pool
You reached through my mantle
And touched me where I was
Created in your image. Brought me off
So gentle, wistful, amused —
And *your* groin all but dead:
Just the thin gruel I would
Coax from the soft old slug
Washing down my skinny wrist.

Old satyr, never lewd — though
Since I left, the earth has dipped
Many times away, through a girl's thighs,
I found last night you only
Brought me to myself
And laughed at us
In the garlic shadowed wood.

You laughed and laughed always
Past your horrors —
Shall my sullen steps ever
Take your bequest that far?

Reedy old Devil, flaunting

The ruin of a massive shoulder,
You were growing back in
Already where the funguses
Stank like my thickening
Semen — your toes splayed
In the forest's groin.

Your bird voice, a ruin too,
Took me past the absurd
And flew through the mad
Echoing brain-pan of one god,
Of two, of a thousand and their prophets
Whose heroes were yours and acknowledged
Only the rotting woods and their own
Rooting ancestors. You laughed
The Grail into being
And silly Merlin stalked wonderfully
Out of your cuff. But you were dead,
And only the nuts mourned,
And your staff was a walking stick
For me which after five years has shivered
Alive in my kitchen last night. . . .

. . . .

I am spoiled, old beauty —
You would not know the armoured
Sexy abstraction I have become.
I fought the world I went to
And won. *You* would have smiled
Through it — "Teach me not
To compete" old crow
Moulting and wise. . . .

. . . .

You and the black queen
Both see beyond the bone man. . . .

. . . .

But which of you wins
In the end? Now I take you up
Again — I have to know.
Did you — will I — go down
Like Merlin? She came to me
Last night after your summons,
And stared at me.
I grinned her out again but though
I grow stronger, every time
It is bluff — will I match her
Ever? She is tight and terribly
Beautiful — I follow *you* down
The loose sleeves of decay,
Afterwards. . . .

. . . .

I tottered into shapes
Of old men, clawed a caricature
Around my rowan staff.
Drunk with senility I wandered
Back — round apple trees clamouring
With voices of the heroic moths.
And the earth beat so hollow
Beneath my feet, my staff. . . .

. . . .

I have inherited
I have inherited
Oh love and age
And careful foolishness.

yesterday

YESTERDAY

This man's shadow
And that man's wife
Came together
On the blade of a knife

One danced out of
A candle flame
And the other threw
Away her name

They drew the bolts
And breathed 'goodnight'
But the dance went on
In the firelight

This man stopped short
In the moon-struck lane
And lost his way
Though his way was plain

The cat looked up
The embers stirred
The shadows closed
Without a word

The frost crept down
Upon the glass
And the man with no shadow
Whispered 'alas'

Shut in the room
The thin ones fell
They kissed and wept
And dreamed of hell

That man's wife
Can never forget
That the candle died
When the knife was wet.

BALTIC

I

When the ice fails
And the world wakes to water
Clamouring like spring birds behind
The rush, drop, drip
Of snow off shuddering spruce sheaves

When the locks have snapped

Go upstream, upstream
Where the gravels hatch out
Chance in the redds of promise. . . .

II

Start now.   In this thaw instant

Do not bolt from the mind's exits to the hotlands of the South.
Refuse the enervated desert of abstractions; reject
The close jungle-sweat of fetish.

Here you know better.

You know that Adam came from ice, thawed and stumbling
Out of a drift; and Eve, a little later,
Stepped from a birch trunk
And ran to him barefoot across the last aconites.

And you have other names for them

And know that Embla-Eve was a girl child only,
Come of a mother who dreamed of Time
Before the world and the north and the ice;
And sent of herself an image, young
In the exuberance of making, twinning
Misleadingly with Adam-Ash.   Who was
But a grudging afterthought.

III

Woman was water

Wrung to the vault strings
Of darkness
She ran down the beating, flat everything,
Willing a tunnel, finding
Herself crouched: a bent
Child-crone screwing her eyes
Tighter and tighter, 'til light burst
Inside her head. She went
In there
Slamming the gate safe.

In her hair forever
A comb of white horn held
The weir of darkness shut.

But Past had issue from that time
And Time was issue of that past.

And only she knows
Who will not know
But stays the tides and brings them
Back into me bruised
By the white horn wall.

She is water and moves
To certain undiscoverable rhythms.

I can say
"She flows"
And I can taste
The cheat of it.

IV

When the world wakes to water
The young night trembles awake:
"Stay with me sweetheart", suddenly

Warm to you again
Under cold Polaris.

Leave her
Now to her lapses, though she cries
Tearfully after you. Set out
And track her constant mother
Still at her high source
In the discarnate sky.

THESE DAYS

Give ground where the moorings split.
I've a parcel of dirt
Too little shrunk
Since you drifted out.

The moon is a child's mummy
Swathed in neglect;
And I am old,
Loose in my windy coat:
Cataract blind,
Stoop and dry to the weather.

These days, planting pebble grits
Piece by piece in the drills
Of my dusty allotment.

THE SEE-SAW TICK-TOCK MAN-POWERED ENGINE

SHE: While I waited
Your hair was winding
Into the old cogs
Of an unpredictable alarm clock.

Next week perhaps
You will be fast;
It will begin to pound
The knells of caution
Upon your eyeballs.

Punctually
I shall have departed.

HE: And I can say
I hate I hate you
Silently
Leaning into the soft
Dumb mouths of your breasts;
Hating and taking
Love that way. Something
Unhinges in my groin and we
Mess together. I ride above the crest.

Below, the lines flicker
Towards each other like tiny
Electric wires on the graph.
They meet, momentarily,
In the mess. Vertiginous
Perhaps, I still ride
The rim of the machine.

IT IS FINISHED

A belt of thorns at land's end
And we are naked of motive,
Having torn through.
        My blood cannot run
        In your wound: At last
You are clutching at cliff flowers
That have no roots.
        Gulls cross below you,
        Love,
        And I would sooner kill you
        Than watch you break
        In the tide.

ANYWAY

This morning a strange new heat
Lay in the clearing.   Insects ticked,
Dust clung to the air's fibres
And roots shook off the crumbling turf.
    I didn't know why I stayed
    Alone in the stifle of our bed
    While you sang back at the crickets.
Until I came out where I understood.
For the two propped mirrors
In your living room
Found their lustre had leaked
Out at the corners.
    Perhaps the trees had wavered
    In the new season's haze,
    Or the spiders had relaxed
    From their tight seclusion,
    Spinning time across the glass.
That was when your face
Began inching tighter
Onto the outline of your skull.
So my drab eyes crept with it.
    Well it's your house, lovely,
    You care for it beautifully.
    And if I prefer waiting
    For a cooler season,
    It's because winter doesn't blossom
    Into such sudden lies.

BIRD IN THE BUSH

This time you're alone —
You don't have to prove
Anything to me.

There are ridiculous symptoms
In my palm. The scars
Are opening up tonight
Like vampires' lids.

How did you find
That the door to leave by
Opens inwards?

I thought my knotty passwords
Would hold. And enough
Unsuspected malice
And muscle to jinx
The exits:

I spied out the thieves' encampment
Of the runway flares. I reckoned
With the flapping red wing light
Carrying you south.

You took another way.
Your furious sadness
Found my own bolt hole.

I have to entertain failures
In my nude front room.
They want to be my brothers
And scrape your power
Off my body. Soon I'll be
Redecorating for their benefit.

We'll brick up the back door
And hammer stakes
Through the pain.

One day you'll be
At the window, wondering
How you ever could have cared.

SEXTET

Reinterpretation

The husks around your feet —
The shards of wings —
Are nothing new. You should
Have come to expect this
By now. But you sit
On your suitcase like a lost
Schoolgirl — as if this
Were the last beach
And the ferry had been scuttled.
Go on, then —
Brood on the debris
Between your toes.
If I were really the devil
I would annihilate your posture
With a laugh.

Girl

Hanging on the tide
With your greasy sails
Flapping like a godmother's skirts,
You have only luck on your side.
  Believe me, she is not
  Omnipotent —
  She too is racked
  By the drawstrings of the moon.
And over here on the sands
The soft slide of surf
Is the white quill-track
Of a hand ruling margins.

'he singeth as he flies'

Look at you, cradling a fire
Against you. Even when

You attend to me, fondling
My dreams with your greenfinch
Eyes, you're crooning
Under your breath
To those famished embers.
Should I put out my hand
To that? I'm tired and shy
Of little mothers whose children
Burn them up and suck me dry.

Behind you

At the blind beach, while I
"I will come back"
Said the cold words
That seemed least to lie;
A black hag
Great with some belly cargo
Beat her wings free of the tides

Her name is Pity, I found later,
After I had fed
Too deep on her endless
White meat.

Plunge

Other, Other,
You are a fish to me:
Cod comfort in my hair.
Oh little foreigner
I pitched my camp
On you after such
A desolate journey.
Why did you fail
So suddenly, why
Did you sink down
Yesterday to those spongy
Reaches? You lie there

As if nothing were changed,
Breathing through your skin.
  Damn you anyway —
You take so much
For granted, but I'm
Gasping for air where
My phantom island
Vanished, and my reasons
Won't hold water.

3:00 a.m.

A black ghost pacing
Jealous under senseless branches,
He mutters the old echo:
The pity of it
Oh the pity
Who is himself an echo
In the echoing woods.

FOX FIRE DIRGE

The year is sick
For the willow moth
Has closed her heart.
She will not wake
Though the year halts by
And his feet are numb
As a leper man's,
For the willow moth
Has closed her heart.

He turns his face
Who must be walking
Though his feet are numb
And the day
Picks at his face.
His seasoned eye
Is crusted over
For the willow moth
Has closed her heart.

Blind to the sun
The sun stands still
For the willow moth
Has closed her heart.
Deaf to the wind
The wind is frozen
For the willow moth
Has closed her heart.

At the still still end
She turns a dream:
To the loose illusion
Of her eyes
The air has grain
And terrors.
She dare not dream

She will not wake
For the willow moth
Has closed her heart.

Snowflake patterned
On his grave:
The year is dead
The dead halt by
Their dreams are numb
The snowflake moth
Enfolded here
Has closed her heart
Has closed her heart
The year is dead
For the willow moth
Has closed her heart.
Has closed her heart.

PISCES

The fish are on a circuit without end
Silver upon woven red
Where the fish leap the sky is red
Where the sky fails them, blood and silver blend.

Clean are the fish and whole, their sides refined
By turning on time's dark wheel
Their silver fins are the rim of the wheel
That turns behind the turnings of your mind.

The wheel spins, half in dark, and then its trace
Leaps across heaven's eye
This is the scale of heaven's eye —
One silver ray, cowled in a hermit's face.

They leap and plunge cold beauties through the sky
Old beyond thought of change
And yet I mark this change
That where men wrote of two fish, three fish fly.

Out of all bounds they mark your destiny
Silver on your red door
Within or without, love, on your door
There, head to tail, your leaping trinity.

equinox

EQUINOX

Where the day splits upon a stone
They watch.   No breath
Informs them, shadows
Of the shadow
Of the stone's dark wedge
Crossing the grass like a knife
Through the dusky red
Scarfing of the mist.

They will watch so,
For patience is their grain
On the cold hill, watch so
For Pleiades' sake, for winter,
For the Hunter's bow.   Profiles
Of lead in the whole and
Oldest shadow, 'til silver
Comes out on them
From the puppet shoals.

They have hearts
Of adamant, cups of
Serpentine, jade
Blades.   And they have
In charge too the hot
And glorious feast of ruby
To drench the stone,
To brim the cups, to
Bring the sun up, to
The keen refinement
Of a scream.

RELEASE

Pressed alive
Between these covers.
Shelved. Too slowly
Dying under the dust seal
Of your conclusions.

The worm turns,
And East by North
By West breathes
And husks tireless
Generations.

Grey specks dart from your hair
By the window: my allies
Mounted on motes
Without shadows. The sun
Choking in the briar hedge
Scarcely notices
The quickening.

At dawn the clasp snaps,
Rusted through,
And my dragon swarm
Storms to your filthy
Vistas. The still sun
Is moonpocked. A million
Wingpricks pare the grey
Dust from your knucklebones.

Only I
Could tread in the various
Sockets of your face
With such patient venom.

WAKE

Since the first moon
Leered on your mother's
Cold shoulder, the tides
Have brought dead things
To garnish your table.

Your appetite sickened
Before their drift.
Picking at the famish
Of a cold child,
Your heart shrank like the last
Discarded apple.

Til I came in
On a dead tide
And laid a gorgeous fruit
At your cramped feet.
Wading in like a hero
From the mist, smiling
Gently over the polished
Skin.

So lightly tricked,
You called me a star,
Lover, magician;
Parted your lips
To my fraud, while I
Splashed back to my craft
On the waking tide.

I knew your tongue
Would taste the worm
Soon enough, but the new
Moon dragged up your face
Against my blade
As I sculled the tide home.

EXORCISM OF THE LETTER J

Then let it always be so
These wide, wide forks at the year's end.

For I know you, I know your ways,
Your stealth through the elder brakes;
I came on you sitting, knee-gazing
In alder shade
But I was hid
In the thickets before you came:
I saw you listen for me
And stake your pose.

So what kind of nymph
Are you? I will not
Loose my first blood
Down your whimsey drain.

Oh the spiders lost under
Your heel, gay reveller,
Know more about your purposes
Than I;
But knowing that's
My amulet. I relate
All faces in my trembling
Stirrup cup
To the grey spinners'
Nest eggs.

Once on your hearth
I showed my horns
And grinned at you
Til your cool eyes flecked
To dismay, and you fled.
I chased you through to your kitchen
And saw you a witch,

High-haunched and footing
Through the shit-littered floor.

I had not seen it before.

Knowing was a hard rush
In my blood, I had you
Stripped.
On the back steps you were
White, and your slim arm
Of a hundred soft hours
Came up at my neck as a rusty axe.

I knocked you down, Jeannie Tap-Tongue,
And while you broke
In slow motion
To the basement floor,
'Pouf' I went
In my own little smoke-cloud
Out through your rooms;

While the vacuum cleaner
And every machine in the place
Cried after me
Like sirens coming down.

NEMESIS

Famine came under the weather:
A thin girl with a curious hunger.

Once she was seen, poised
And cool in a country club bar.
Then a glimpse of her face
Languorous in the wind
Of a rich boy's sports car,
Racing at 2:00 am. to the lanes
And promptings of the New Forest.

She was noticed after a while
In several cities
And then she was everywhere . . .

'Til all the girls in the slums
And on the streets, in the stores
And at last in cottages
Wore her face.

'Til matrons and widows
And ladies with bloated
Unlovely skin, breathed with
Her curious catch of breath,
Trimmed to her figure.

The hospital wards were full
Of her, paler than the pillows,
Charging the starched sheets
With a she-wolf's hunger.

And everywhere the men came
As never before to their women.
And little girls shot up and
Maneens rutted like satyrs,
'Til the wasting ivy lust
Worked every man to his listless
Ends. Paralysis. The skinny twine

Of her wrists worked and coaxed
Our weary shoulder blades
And in the last hungover dawn
A grey smile surfaced around
Her bright lamprey eyes, before
She sank out of our ken, and gone,
The weather too late returned.

LUCK

It seems the lady and I
At last
Have parted company.
Only the ghost
Of a laugh in the rhododendrons
Where the driveway bends
And the secret green doors
Are sealed by dusty flowers

Echoes and echoes and echoes

I was so sure of her:
I carried her favours
In my eyelids. And the crows'
Feet wrung them dry.

So now I falter
Dizzied by where and why
The boy who suddenly wakes
Walker
In cramped spaces
Among all men's tracks

It comes to this
I am not immune
I am not immune
Sometimes I am
A blind passenger
In a car spinning, spinning
Out on an icy corner.

It is the way, always,
When she leaves. Santa Maria,
I see Columbus wrecked:
Tipped on the rocks and hanging
Over the long long pouring
Fall into chaos.

My daughters have her ear
For a little while:
Guardian angel, stay near
The uncareful child.

I fold lures for her in the snow
And the traps are sprung
Each morning
The delicate faultless footprints
Circle and circle

To the quick of the aspens surely
She will shift her lair
If I go out to her
One night
Quite naked
Will she be fair?

REVENANT

Who are you, dark artisan,
Holding me again?
I know your touch.
Every time you put me aside
I sink back into the cold
Drift of things.
Then I hear other stones
Cracking under your driftwood
Fire, and your dark
Hand reaches into the shadows
And finds me.
Why do you turn me til the heat
Of your hand and the heat
Of your fire scores into me?
Your eye bores in with the warmth
Your dark eye considers me.
I think you hold iron
In your left hand —
I am hot and afraid.   Throw me
Back into the shadows
And let me be a dead thing
In the cold tides and winds.
  What do you want
  On this last beach
  With fire and iron
  And auger eyes?
  Who are you, black pilgrim?
I think that soon
You will know my grain
To a fault.   The fire
Will flare in your black eyes
And your left hand strike.
When I have shattered
You will go inland
With my heart.

OLD COUNTRY

Into the sea-sound
A rising whisper;
Aroar on the hob
From the turf-smoked
Stones.
From every cottage door
Old voice muttering
The East! The East's at war
Old house listening
From all about the city walls
Sea and kettle
In a roaring
Boil.
          the border's lost
Water unclouding
In the tumid kettle
His withered hand gives no command
Rippling silent
As the sea beats
Round.
          ruled fitly here
Your eyes catch mine
Past my old grandmother
Seven queens I've led to my royal bed
Singing alone
While the young ones
Wait.
Until an heir was born,
But now my crown
                              I think you are listening
As I am watching
An old face at the door
The eyes and the hand
That were passed to
Me.

the hag of the moor.
Old one bending
To fill the teapot
Shall fetch you back your youth
The last in this place
Where the sea takes
All.
has cast his robe aside
And naked as a babe
Bathes in the brew and drinks it too
We have returned
Of our generation
And all drew back again
From a broken bond
To this island
Life,
Seeking our parents'
Rejected portion
With ne'er a word to his queen he's spurred
Out through the eastern gate.
And pass some knowledge
Down with our
Blood.
my young king shall come
And turn that host away.
Your ears and my eyes
And the thin voice singing
Throng these old walls
But arrow straight towards the gate
The shining vanguard rides.
In a moment's
Spell.
Each from this moment
Shall take an emblem
A sapling shoot by the toppled root
Of a grey withered tree.
From the bothey, the sea,

And the frozen
Time.
our king's returned
Leading our eastern foe
The windspray flecks
On the hollowed doorstep
He's broken through the gatemen
You turn your knees
To the settling
Flames.
He's let the blood of those who stood
Guarding the royal stair
Old hand reaches
For golden softness,
Rests on your head
She leaps up ghostly pale;
Her gown is tossed
As mine has
Done.
Her maids weep in the hall.
Smiling together
though scarcely acknowledged,
the victors sing
'Tis you shall wear the crown.
We rise and assist
Til the table's
Set,
Out at the narrow western gate
They go throughout that night,
Turning our backs
To the doors and shutters
For mothers dragged their wailing bairns
Seated again
But of the old the worst is told
By the forbears'
Fire,
We marvel at every

Forceful deftness
The fair queen must be found —
She shall abide to be the bride
Of the dry fingers
Voice and form.
Turning around
With scones and teapot,
She looks at my eyes
She's wrapped herself in gypsy guise
And crossed the eastern plain;
Within her womb there stirs the doom
Shall break the walls again.
And pours our
Tea.

NIGHTWOOD

Where the death's head moth
Tugs at the bark, it is still.
A pale half-moon has gone
To waste, but scratching
The mites scribble daft
Lines on the tree
Between
The moth's padding feet.

And the mites in the dead
Leaves below, crawl into
The eyes of a drying thrush.

"There is lime on the branches"
Whispers the stiff beak, "and lime
On my tongue. I scraped it off
Where the old moth hides
Her eggs, and the stuff
Took root in the wood
And among my feathers. I fell
Under this swinging shadow
A week ago."
"But wait,"
Called the ants swarming by,
"Wait for the berries, throstle,
And the moonwax again
On your brothers' beaks."

"That shadow will stretch
When it has swung enough."
So the dark mandrake was breathing
In the turn of night. "There will always
Be wax enough, and tallow and lime
And time enough in this place."

QUALICUM

. . . So you will find upon the warm wet
Orchid-hoarding moss pads,
Like a great Celtic brooch
In the rain belt sprawling
Or Brigit's firewheel cross
A tree upended.

Hard in its clay-gripped clasp
The writhing root-medallion
Clenches a stone. Regard it,
For in Time's sifting fashion
The earthstone, refaceted
As distant dawns require,
Outfaces every setting.

The thin suns' philtres
Shall freeze the mosses here
While the rimed stone sparkles;
But the drowning under
The steaming coral suns
And the drought below
The broad sun's scrutiny
Shall change this place.

When wash and weathering
Have ground away the span
Of eye and root and leaf,
The shrunken stone shall
Almost perfectly
Pulse on the desert
With a new-born light.

UNDER CHAC'S EYES

Garza the Heron
Stalked in the shallows
Where the chaco steamed
Away into summer.

Garza saw the scorched
Peeling dead back
Of Manguruyu crawling
Gill-deep to nowhere.

Two moons past only
In the spilling river
Garza, splay-feathered,
Would have gone down,
Flapping ungainly
To the gravy bottom
With the great catfish
Clamped to his leg.

Now Garza pokes
A mincing spear-beak
And breaks off a crumb
From the grey, grilled back;

Tasting, reflecting
In his grey eyed patience,
Then he lunges and gouges
Flesh from the gills.

Manguruyu, a life now
But no more, no fish,
Crawls, threshes a little,
Wet-bellies further.

Garza stilt dances,
Dabbing for a sweet fry
Here and there, then returning
To his man-length meal.

Chicuelo saw this,
Vaquero, slack-reined
On the hillside, waiting
For Pablo's Maria.

DEFEAT

I see peace is a vulture
Flapping down the bleached
Pasture: spoiling all
And mousey looters pick through
The stench. We turn
To talk of marriages,
To rive gilt rings
Through a dungeon stone.
Should I know
Or care what I have signed?
My side is stiffening
Yet I yawn, or perhaps
The wings that bat the sun
Distract me. It is written
Truce is a season
Of paupers, and indeed
My faithful, unsteady mercenaries
Are stragglers now. Stay
Or go with them — at their backs
My seed is dogged
By the heirs of carrion.

CANTATION

Seven, seven, sorrow and sigh
Firs upstretched before the sky
Muzzles tearing at the moon
Taut dark neck-fur starkly tuned
Seven, seven, sorrow and sigh
Here the sea wind's dogged cry
Through the tendon, branch and bark
Gutters moonbeams in the dark
Seven, seven, sorrow and sigh
Packs of clouds quarter the sky
  Seven clouds to drown the light
  Seven winds to rend the night
  Seven waves in the windy cove
  Seven years for our hunted love.

ELEMENTAL

Make no mistake of this
I
am the name maker.

  Alright! Look up —
I'm here
in the ragged shower of dust and ash
come down on your hair.
My home this winter season
is the apple-tree's crutch.

None of that, now:
you won't catch me
in any hold-all net
of mythology.

> I am the phantom pain
> in a severed arm;
> I am the worm in your tooth,
> wrecking your speculations;
> I am the Crab,
> my sign is scored on your door:
> Bring out your dead.
> Bring out your nameless dead.

This suits me
lazing under the dome
of a magpie's nest.
It may look windy,
this swaying tick and tack
of fibred ash twigs,
but I have named it comfort
and I lie easy.

> I am the brute mirror
> in the zoo-ape's eye;
> the clashing of dead branches

across the paddock;
A boy crying 'wolf'
at the nursery window.

If you took the wind on your face
and climbed in these crusty branches,
shredding your cuffs, staining
your knees with lichen,
You'd find me
a pookish sort of fellow
just now,
but, for you, not comfortable.

The tan of my skin
drawn taut as a boat's hull
across my bones
stirring, oh yes, the dusty vault
of memory.   Afterwards
you would think

"Out of a mummy's wrappings,
that skin, out of the peat bog . . . "
or the old puff-ball you kicked
in Deepdale woods.

And then I am like the troll with no back:
You would not remember my eyes.

I take a certain
interest in people

I am the call
floating
from an orchard swing;

The song's full measure
crooned
in the tenement yard;

I name them the same
the white girl, the wino;

I am in them both
tasting no difference

That's why I choose
the magpie's nest.

The birds fan on round wings
over the village, crying
chakka,chakka,chakka
Every one is someone's grand-
or great-grand-father;
a whole brood of ancestors
hatched this year
from my nest here. Off they flew.
One got shot by the keeper
and nailed up with the stoats
in his larder. The rest stay.

Not a louse in the Nazarene's beard
but I had a name for it:
Streicher, Speeler, and Grout . . .
one of them is with me here
in the filthy lambswool pad
of my pie's nest. I have
changed her name . . .

I am the wild shadow
at your shoulder
racing down the staircase

I am the sudden crouch
in the booming nettle patch

So I *do* take a certain
interest in people —
while they last.
The point is:
Things are not forgotten
Just because people forget them.

They batten on the seeds
of my world. It's me
that whispers their names
when the wind is right.

I am the father's shaking rage
when his baby cries and cries
and looks at him from other eyes
and screams at him.

I am the impulse to kick the dog.

I live in the spaces:
look for me
through the windows
men call shadows.

Now,
here's one story:

'A sort of man came this way,
walking in the fall. Our tricky
Indian sun was gentling
the warm rocks and he chose
this tree. Soon, tip-necked
against the jig-saw bark,
he softly snored, and I
bird-fashion hopped
across the afternoon
and picked out with my black beak
a little worm thing from his head.

chakka chakka chakka chakka
he has never found out. . . .'

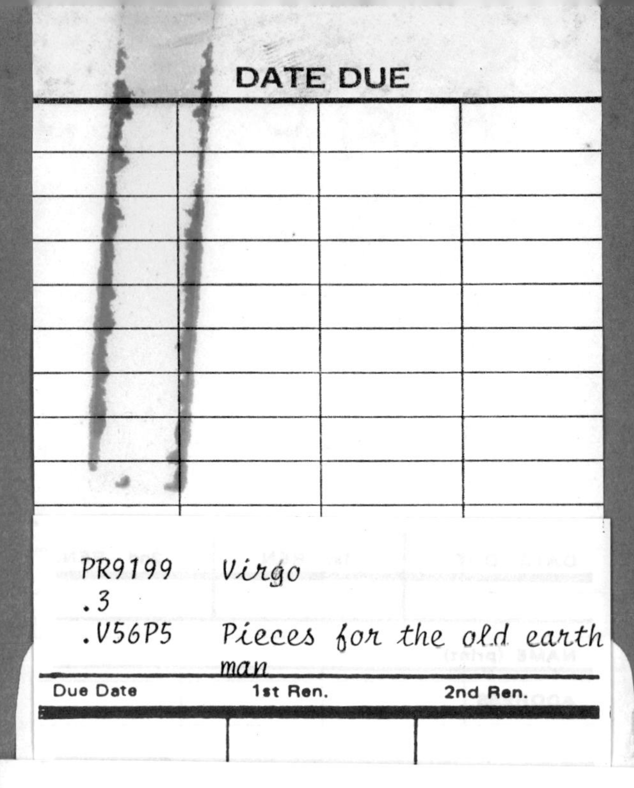
DATE DUE
PR9199
.3
.V56P5
Virgo
Pieces for the old earth man
Due Date
1st Ren.
2nd Ren.